UNDERSTANDING YOURSELF AND YOUR RELATIONSHIPS

Notes from a Therapist's Desk

HALLIE FRANK, PH.D.

For my grandchildren: Benjamin, Jillian, Allison, Talia, Aaron, Noah, Kaia, Ellie, Benny, Sydney, and Sammy.

Contents

PART I

Introduction

1

Who I am

I am a 76-year-old clinical psychologist with over fifty years of clinical experience. I was born to Jewish parents in Montreal, Canada, where I have lived my entire life. My childhood was not an easy one. When I was 6 years old, my younger brother was diagnosed with childhood autism. My loving parents, who were devastated by the diagnosis, engaged in an endless search for treatments, all of which proved profoundly disappointing. To intensify my mother's distress, the primary determinant of autism, according to the medical establishment at the time, was a "refrigerator mother"[1]. Leo Kanner introduced the notion that autism was a consequence of frigid, detached mothering, an idea elaborated upon by Bruno Bettelheim. As the healthy child in the family, I often felt that it was incumbent on me to be as "normal" as possible to repair my parents' wounded self-esteem. My normality allowed them to show the world and the numerous professionals who treated my brother that his condition did not arise from defective parenting. In my view, moreover, my parents' intense pride in my academic success mitigated their deep feelings of shame about my brother's abnormal behavior.

I have been married twice. I was devastated when my first marriage ended after twenty-four reasonably good years. I was on my own for seven somewhat difficult years. At 52, I met my present husband, a widower at 53, at a bridge club. We are fortunate to have shared a nourishing, sustaining relationship for over twenty-four years.

I have one daughter and two sons as well as two step-sons, all of whom have married (one is recently divorced) and have had children. Although only one of those families lives in Montreal, we are committed to maintaining close contact with our children by means of phone calls, visits, and regular family get-togethers on religious holidays and vacations. Nevertheless, I am somewhat envious of friends whose children live in the same city and can see their fami-lies on a more casual, spontaneous basis. I enjoy extremely close relationships with my own children despite the initially unsettling aftermath of the divorce. In addition, I am delighted that my husband's sons have welcomed me into their lives and that his daughters-in-law, who never met his first wife, have embraced me as a mother-in-law and grandmother for their children. My husband and I share eleven grandchildren ranging in age from 9 to 19. I was somewhat amazed to discover the passion I feel about my grandchildren and the degree to which I enjoy being a grandmother.

As I am a natural extrovert, my friends and extended family have always played a major role in my life. Despite the constraints imposed by time and distance, some of my friendships have endured for over sixty years. Others were forged during my years as an undergraduate or graduate student. As a parent of young children, I also developed relationships with other parents, some of which have remained lasting friends. During the throes of my divorce, my friends and family were there for me in ways that made a crucial difference for my mental health. With increasing age and decreasing time and energy, I have become somewhat more discriminating about friendships. Nevertheless, I have discovered the importance of tolerance for others' frailties and the insight that no person has to function as an all-purpose friend.

Two additional details involving bridge and books are central to my story. I am a passionate, competitive, perhaps addicted player of duplicate bridge. Through that pastime, I have acquired a few close friends as well as many delightful and not-so-delightful acquaintances. Bridge, played at a competitive level, can be both emotionally and intellectually stressful. Most players of duplicate bridge take the game very seriously and strive to excel (i.e., win). Among these serious strivers is a number of men and women whose self-esteem seems to be wrapped up in the game. Over the years, I have encountered several brilliant people who, for a variety of reasons, did not achieve intellectual fulfillment through their careers. As a result, bridge became the primary vehicle for asserting their intellectual superiority. These individuals often become irrationally angry, lambasting their partners and opponents for mistakes that compromise their own achievements. People like me who are critical of their own errors take to heart unsolicited criticism from others.

I also belong to a book club that has been meeting for over thirty years and which, in many ways, functions as a women's support group. We often discuss our personal lives in addition to books and have shared the joys of many happy milestones such as the marriage of children and the birth of grandchildren. We have also supported each other through personal challenges such as children's divorces, grandchildren with disabilities, the death of spouses and elderly parents, as well as age-related concerns about health. Sadly, one of our beloved members passed away two years ago.

I have always been an interested observer of human nature. My high school yearbook caption reads "experience is that which causes us to make the same mistake in a different way". At 17 years of age, I have no idea what experience I was drawing on to generate these words of wisdom. My listed ambition was "to be a social worker (solving other people's problems)," and my probable destination was "not being able to solve her own".

For many years, I was Chief Clinical Psychologist at the McGill University Mental Health Service. In addition, I worked in the clinical psychology department at Concordia University, where I conducted graduate-level seminars on theoretical models of behavior change as well as supervisory groups on short-term therapy. I have always maintained a part-time private practice. My primary therapeutic orientation is psychodynamic. This approach encourages clients to recognize and examine the reasons for repetitive behavior patterns, to appreciate their own contributions to these patterns, and to understand the possible motives of significant others. In clinical jargon, this is referred to as a "revised perspective".

2

Why I wrote this book

It has been my good fortune to have abundant personal relationships and fruitful interactions with colleagues, students, supervisees, and clients of different ages who have sought help for a wide range of problems. In addition, personal experiences at the bridge club provided a rich arena for observations of human nature.

As I have grown older and perhaps wiser, conversations with clients, friends, and colleagues have often prompted my reiteration of perspectives about the difficulties people experience as a result of their dynamics, as if these observations contained fundamental truths that I could share. This collection of essays is based on these reflections about human nature. It is not intended as a scholarly work. Nevertheless, some essays draw heavily on formal psychological theory in addition to insights derived from interactions with clients, family, friends, and bridge partners. I avoid psychological jargon where possible, and I explain psychological concepts in everyday language. In other essays, which are based solely on my own observations, I have taken the liberty of offering personal opinions that are not as grounded in psychological theories.

Unfortunately, we are often blind to personal missteps that seem transparent when observed in others. My primary goal in this volume is to illuminate some of the blind spots that promote or prolong emotional pain and its consequences. It's like having a whispering therapist in your ear, one who prompts you to reflect on your foibles, past and present, and those of others. A secondary goal is to provide the kinds of insights for therapists that I would have valued early in my professional career.

Each essay touches on a unique aspect of human nature and how it affects our relationships. Some of the essays focus largely on individual dynamics, whereas others focus on relationships, although the two are often inextricably linked. I hope to provide readers with a better understanding of their own and others' motives, offering practical suggestions for managing painful emotions and difficult relationships. Where possible, I note how therapeutic work can address these concerns. This volume would provide useful insights to those who are considering therapy or potential changes in their current therapeutic direction. Therapists, whether novice or experienced, will also appreciate the descriptions of individual and relationship dynamics as well as the illustrative anecdotes.

PART II

Individual Dynamics

On repetitive patterns: why we keep making the same mistakes

We often unwittingly repeat the same patterns of self-defeating behavior, as Sigmund Freud termed *the repetition compulsion*[2]. According to Freud, we repeat these behaviors, hoping for more favorable outcomes in subsequent instances, or what he referred to as *belated mastery of the original trauma*[3]. Other scholars have proposed alternative explanations for repetitive behavior patterns[4].

In general, we react to current problems through the lens of our past experience. As a result, we may perceive a threat that is irrelevant to our current circumstances. Due to heightened anxiety, we avoid the seemingly threatening situation, missing an opportunity to learn that the threat is no longer realistic.

Psychologists Neil Miller and John Dollard generated similar avoidant behavior in rats[4]. The rats learned to avoid a neutral stimulus after repeatedly receiving a painful electric shock in the presence of that stimulus. Because the rats continued to avoid the stimulus long after the shocks had ceased, they had no opportunity to unlearn their previous response of avoidance and agitation.

In analogous fashion, a number of my female clients have exhibited a phobic avoidance of men. Those who grew up with tyrannical, verbally abusive fathers became anxious around men and consistently avoided them, which prevented them from learning that most men are not at all like their fathers. These women never dated, instead fulfilling their need for companionship through intense friendships with single women. Over time, as their friends found partners, they became increasingly isolated and lonely.

Another explanation for repetitious patterns is that our way of being in the world, which originates in childhood interactions with parents, elicits responses from others that perpetuate previous interpersonal experiences. In other words, in line with Paul Wachtel's *cyclical psychodynamic* perspective, in our current relationships, we inadvertently replicate our old unsatisfying interactions[5].

For example, children who have experienced non-nurturing childhoods assume a stance of pseudo-independence: "I don't have to depend on anybody, I'll depend on myself". As adults, they exhibit a competent, autonomous exterior that signals their unwillingness to depend on others. Resultantly, they are deprived of the everyday dependency gratification (e.g., getting appropriate help from others) that is available to most of us in adulthood. Because people in their milieu view them as competent as well as standoffish, they are unlikely to offer ordinary help. That way of being in the world, which was adaptive in a non-nurturing childhood context, results in continued non-fulfillment of their dependency needs.

One of my friends recently recounted related difficulties he was experiencing with his adult daughter. This daughter always felt that she had received a raw deal in childhood because of her parents' marital difficulties. Her way of being in the world, which was to reproach others for not proving their devotion, affected her relationships with her now older parents as well as her partner. Despite her parents' and her partner's devotion to her practical and emotional needs, she became irrationally angry at the most minor of missteps. Her bitter complaints resulted in their withdrawal, which recreated the original situation in which she felt abandoned and uncared for.

Yet another explanation concerns our choice of friends and partners. Because familiarity is comforting, we are inclined to gravitate towards people who remind us of significant figures in our past, including those with whom we had dysfunctional interactions. Our gravitation toward the familiar has parallels to *filial imprinting* in non-human species, as described by Douglas Spalding and Konrad Lorenz, and *sexual imprinting*, as documented by James Galligher [6, 7, 8]. Birds and mammals become strongly attached to (i.e., imprint on) the first moving object they are exposed to during early life, regardless of its properties (even if it is inanimate). Moreover, male birds attempt to mate with females from the species that raised them (i.e., foster mothers) rather than females from their own species (i.e., biological mothers). The implication for humans is that phenomena like filial and sexual imprinting could influence our interpersonal and sexual preferences as adults. Sexual imprinting, in particular, might affect the sought-after characteristics in potential mates.

Upon meeting a new person, people often remark, "I feel as if I have known them all my life". Such comments usually refer to positive, familiar attributes of an important person from the past. We run into difficulty, however, when we choose people who embody familiar but negative traits of past significant others. For example, some of my female clients with emotionally unavailable parents repeatedly choose emotionally unavailable men, presumably because of the comfort initially generated by the feelings of familiarity.

Familiarity-based feelings of comfort can also extend to other important relationships such as those with employers or supervisors. A poignant example involved a graduate student who sought therapy for depression generated by difficulties with her male doctoral supervisor. The supervisor was inconsistent and unreliable about providing funds for her scientific research. At times, the student would order equipment that her supervisor had previously approved, only to learn subsequently of insufficient funds for the expenditure. This generated considerable stress and embarrassment. Because she grew up with an unpredictable and financially irresponsible father, she did not initially recognize her supervisor's behavior as inappropriate. Instead, she responded to the familiar chaos by apologetically trying to compensate for her supervisor's behavior in much the same way that she had responded previously to her father's financially irresponsible behavior.

A final and less psychological explanation for repeated behavior patterns relates to our temperament, much of which is biologically determined. Heraclitus, the Greek philosopher, wrote that "character is destiny". It follows that our way of being in the world leads us into repetitive patterns of relationships with others. This provides a partial explanation of why certain children are resilient in the face of circumstances of early harsh deprivation and abuse. Their naturally engaging temperament serves as a protective factor in eliciting positive responses from teachers, coaches, or other adults. These parental surrogates provide them with the personalized responsiveness, mentoring, and protection that buffer them from developmental disruption.

A therapist can help clients become aware of these recurring patterns and their origins. Some of the aforementioned factors may be simultaneously at play. If it is a simple case of past-present confusion, the therapist can foster clients' understanding that they are overreacting to the present in terms of the past. An additional step is to help clients interrupt the cycle of avoidance to truly understand that their anxiety is unwarranted. In cases where clients are unwittingly provoking present situations to replicate the past, the therapist can help them identify and work on changing their own contributions to the dysfunctional patterns. When clients choose partners whose negative characteristics resemble those of past significant figures, the therapeutic work revolves around an examination of whether the current relationship can be changed and is worth salvaging or whether leaving a dysfunctional relationship is feasible and preferable. As most therapists are aware, there are gratifying aspects to the most emotionally abusive relationships. The role of the therapist is to help clients identify the toxic and rewarding parts of the relationship, also helping them to articulate their ambivalent feelings. The goal is for the client to make more empowered decisions about whether to stay in or leave their relationships.

4

On envy

Envy is one of our most pernicious emotions. When relationships deteriorate, it is often because one of the participants is envious of the other and expresses it in a destructive way. At times, the object of the envy does not recognize what is occurring and feels deeply wounded. Envy can be elicited by any number of attributes such as material possessions, personal characteristics such as intellect, beauty, and a likeable personality, or a nurturing family. In my experience, however, what triggers the most intense feelings of envy is the natural confidence that some people possess in abundance.

As human beings, we have several ways of managing our envious feelings. The most healthy and constructive way is to admit to ourselves that we feel jealous and then to strategize how to acquire for ourselves what we envy in others. Accomplishing this goal depends, first, on tolerating the uncomfortable emotion of envy and, subsequently, on having good enough self-esteem to imagine that we are also deserving of what we envy. At times, it is also helpful if we can openly admit our jealous feelings to the other person rather than allowing our envy to be shown in more indirect and destructive ways. For example, a teenage girl might envy her friend's popularity and strategize how to expand her own social circle.

There are other less constructive responses to envy which result in either a passive or active destruction of relationships. The destructive nature of envy is central to a number of literary works. In Ian McEwan's gripping novel *Atonement*, the younger sister is so jealous of her older sister that she tells a lie that changes the course of their lives[12].

The most benign solution is to avoid the envied person because any interaction reminds us of what we lack. Consider a woman who, after many failed attempts to get pregnant, learns that her best friend has effortlessly become pregnant. She might distance herself from her friend and refuse to attend the baby shower because to do so would trigger intense feelings of jealousy.

A second and more destructive way of handling envious feelings is the so-called "sour grapes" phenomenon whereby we devalue what we envy[9]. In the original fable, the fox, unable to reach for the desired grapes, decides that he really does not want them because the grapes are probably sour[9]. In her seminal essay, "Envy and Gratitude", Melanie Klein refers to this defence as "envious spoiling"[10]. In similar fashion, we might envy a friend for their popularity, consoling ourselves with the notion that to be that popular would interfere with our studies. Simply put, we denigrate the desired characteristics to make ourselves feel better about not having them.

Sometimes, these rationalizations have a grain of truth and serve an adaptive purpose. For example, I have known people with traumatic childhoods who tell themselves that coping with adversity made them stronger so that they do not envy their friends' nurturing and protective families.

This is partially true, but it can also be seen as making a virtue out of necessity. In reality, it does not mean that they would not have wanted more supportive families.

The third, most primitive, and most destructive way of handling envy is to eliminate the object of envy. Melanie Klein calls this response "envious robbing"[10]. In the mind of the envious person, "since I can't have it, you won't have it either". In that vein, if a teenage girl is envious of her best friend's popularity, she might spread vicious lies about her to common friends or exclude her from social gatherings, thereby destroying her friend's social status. The popularity of social media has increased the ease of destroying reputations (e.g., posting compromising pictures) or generating feelings of exclusion (e.g., posting pictures of get-togethers). One of my granddaughters was saddened when she learned on social media that she had been excluded from several social functions despite being one of the most proficient members of her sports team. I also recall having several personal experiences of this nature. One painful experience occurred when I was 13. My best friend at the time abruptly turned on me and succeeded in alienating me from our circle of friends. I was dejected for the rest of the school year and buried myself in books. Reflecting on it from an adult perspective, I can conjecture that she was jealous of my superior academic status. Despite her considerable effort and intellectual abilities, she was unable to surpass my academic achievements. Perhaps more important was her chaotic family life and secret sorrow that I learned about much later— sexual abuse by her music teacher. My stable and supportive family, despite its aura of sadness, probably exacerbated her envy.

As the targets of envy, regardless of its manifestations, we are not always aware of what is happening. That was certainly the case with my 13-year-old self. I was only aware of feeling sad, excluded, and deeply flawed. We are less likely to recognize the manifestations of envy in other people if we are not envious people ourselves and, therefore, are less likely to attribute envious motives to others.

The destructive nature of envy is reflected in superstitions that span cultures and historical periods. Frederick Thomas Elworthy compiled legends on the curse of the evil eye, which involves the belief that people who achieve success invoke the envy of those around them. This is thought to bring about a reversal of fortunes, a curse transmitted by an evil glare[11]. In many cultures, people wear hidden amulets (with a visible eye) to ward off the envy of others. Likewise, I have known several successful professionals who avoid talking about their achievements for fear of inviting bad luck (i.e., invoking the evil eye) as if the envy of others might reverse or attenuate their good fortune.

As therapists, we sometimes focus on helping clients understand that a deteriorating relationship might stem from being the object of envious feelings. Initially, clients are usually convinced that they are the sole cause of the dissolution of their relationship. As therapists, we are of course aware that envy is not the only explanation, and clients are encouraged to examine their own contributions to failed relationships. At times, however, the envy of others is the most viable explanation. This perspective, when warranted, helps to restore the client's self-esteem.

5

On authenticity

All of us long to be truly known and valued. That is partly why we feel best when we are a part of a community in which people know us personally. This is one of the advantages of living in a small town, participating in a religious community, or holding membership in a recreational club.

Some people manage to live what can be termed a "double-life". The most extreme example involves bigamists who have two families, neither aware of the other. Other examples are long-term affairs or relationships that are kept secret from family and friends. Such people experience a deep sense of inauthenticity because they cannot be truly known by significant people in their everyday lives.

A salient example in my clinical practice was a client who was unusually close to her immigrant family. Because of her fear of their intrusiveness, she was unable to tell them about her long-term, live-in relationship with a partner from a different background. Her failure to integrate those two compartmentalized lives left her beset by constant feelings of dysphoria and anxiety.

I have also worked with several female clients who, despite being in long-term relationships, engaged in emotional and/or physical affairs with other men. They characterized their partners as stable and reliable but boring individuals. In addition to providing novel sexual interest, these affairs allowed for deep and interesting conversation of which their partners were incapable. As long as the relationships remained clandestine, these women described a sense of profound alienation from people in their lives. Unable to tolerate these feelings, some of the women eventually confided in close female friends or, in some cases, their long-term partners. Despite the guilt about hurting their husbands or the shame of being perceived as morally bankrupt, their moods improved substantially when they stopped leading double lives.

One of my clients remained paralyzed, unable to tell her partner or her lover about the other's existence. Not only did she have deep fears of hurting either man, but she was also avoiding the intense grief of relinquishing either of these important relationships. As a result, she remained chronically dysphoric, largely because of her inauthentic life where she could not be truly known in either of her most important relationships.

Aside from the dysphoria engendered by compartmentalization, there are other ramifications of a double life that revolve around loss (illness or death) involving the secret partner. I have known of instances in which an entirely unknown person cries uncontrollably at a funeral. A secret lover is unable to mourn the loss publicly, leaving family and friends of this person confused by the abrupt onset of grief-like dysphoria with no apparent target of grief. These cases are examples of what Kenneth Doka has termed *disenfranchised grief*— grief that is not openly acknowledged, socially accepted, or publicly mourned[13]. Because the relationship is not recognized, there can be no recognition of the loss and associated grief.

If the secret life is suddenly exposed, there are severe emotional consequences in the form of betrayal and shock for family and friends of the deceased person. Many years ago, I worked with a university student who sought therapy after becoming aware that her father had an entire family in a different country. As the youngest daughter in the original family, she always felt as if she occupied a special place in her father's affections. She was heartbroken to learn that he had another daughter in his second family who was younger than her, stimulating intense feelings of betrayal and jealousy.

I also knew someone who visited his father weekly at his rented apartment after his parents' divorce. The son noticed the lack of furniture and largely empty closets, but he did not make much of it at the time because he was very young. Upon his father's sudden death, he and his mother were devastated to learn that the father had never lived in that apartment, which was kept solely for his son's visits. In fact, his father had lived for years with his closeted gay lover in a large, opulent house in another neighborhood. Ultimately, a lack of authenticity can be extremely detrimental, and in therapy, one can work towards presenting a truer version of the self.

6

On guilt: neurotic or warranted

Traditional dynamic theories hypothesize that guilt arises from parents' prohibition of a child's natural impulses such as sex and aggression[14]. The child is thought to internalize these prohibitions in their conscience, feeling guilty whenever these impulses are stirred up. Freud referred to these impulses as the *id* and the conscience as the *super-ego*[14]. In order to have a civilized society, it is necessary to have a mechanism for limiting the uncontrolled expression of our base instincts. Parents serve as a conduit for larger societal prohibitions, and religion plays a role as exemplified in codifications of religious law, as in the Bible or the Koran.

Our ability to feel guilty is adaptive for civil society. However, in some family, religious, or cultural traditions, children are made to feel more than the usual amount of guilt about their impulses, resulting in irrational or neurotic guilt. Therapy helps affected clients recognize that the intensity of their guilt about normal impulses is not warranted.

It is important to distinguish between irrational or neurotic guilt and justifiable guilt, the latter involving situations in which we hurt another physically or emotionally. If someone steals from their business partner, the valid emotional response is to feel guilty, and a healthy reaction is reparation (e.g., returning the money). In some situations, reparation may not be possible. A constructive response would be to learn from one's mistake and resolve not to repeat the transgression.

A non-constructive response to guilt is to engage in ceaseless self-flagellation. One of my clients felt extremely guilty after cheating on her partner. She became extremely depressed and tormented herself with endless self-reproach. Our work together revolved around allowing her to acknowledge her genuine guilt but helping her understand that continually lambasting herself was not productive and that her energy could be used more constructively to learn from her mistakes and to resolve to remain faithful in the future.

On being an exception

There is a narcissistic kernel in the least grandiose of us that causes us to secretly believe that we are so special as to merit being an exception. This belief can lead us to make poor choices in relationships. We might observe our partners mistreating other people, but we believe that because we are so special and therefore the exception, our partners would never treat us in this fashion.

The tendency to consider ourselves as exceptions is more marked in the young. With age, I have come to realize the folly in thinking that we are ever the exception. If we observe someone mistreating others, sooner or later that nastiness will be directed towards us.

The truth is that the best predictor of present behavior is past behavior. I have often asked clients who sought help for issues of betrayal if there were any red flags that could have alerted them to the eventual deterioration of their relationship. On further reflection, they often mentioned that their partners had previously betrayed other partners.

One flagrant example is women whose partners leave their previous wives for them and are subsequently unfaithful to them. The women naïvely think of themselves as special, the exception, and more lovable than the previous wives. They are devastated by their partners' infidelity, which seems entirely predictable from an outside vantage point.

Likewise, I have learned that if a client who seeks my help has been dissatisfied with several previous therapists, I can expect to be next on the chopping block. Early in my career, I referred a dissatisfied and somewhat pathological client to a highly experienced therapist. About a year later, I was dumbfounded to receive a call from this colleague, who offered an apology. He disclosed his expectation, when accepting the referral, of being more successful with the client than I was because of my relative inexperience. Upon entering his office, the client attempted to throw him in the air. He became aware that she was so deeply disturbed as to necessitate hospitalization. He apologized for his arrogance, thinking that he was the exception rather than paying attention to my experience with the client and using it as a cautionary tale.

On holding a grudge

There are a number of wise old sayings about holding grudges. One of my favorites (unknown author) is that holding a grudge is like letting a person live rent-free in your head. The Buddha countenanced that "holding onto anger is like drinking poison and expecting the other person to die". Barbara Johnson quipped that "grudges are like hand grenades; it is wise to release them before they destroy you".

Some people become permanently embittered after being wronged. They obsess about their hurt and betrayal and fantasize about revenge. In some cases, they might actually act out their vengeful fantasies. It becomes so important to exact revenge on the betrayer that they do not consider that the ramifications of their behavior may have profound personal costs.

An example I encountered early in my clinical practice was of a young man who was furious at his domineering, narcissistic father who co-opted his son's success as his own. This client rebelled by deliberately doing poorly in all of his university courses. When it came time to embark on a career four years later, he was devastated to learn that he did not have the grades for admission to any professional program. In therapy, he became aware that his preoccupation with defeating his father was in fact self-defeating, and he had only succeeded in hurting himself.

In another example, I have known divorced women who were so hurt by what they experienced as their husbands' betrayal that they endlessly sought revenge by repeatedly renegotiating the custody and financial arrangements. In many divorce agreements, it is frequently the father who is financially responsible for big-ticket items such as the children's education. I knew one divorced couple where the wife repeatedly chose the most expensive private school in an attempt to bankrupt her husband. Had her former husband refused to pay for this school, he would have appeared, in the eyes of his children, insufficiently supportive of a quality education for them.

I have known others who constructed blatant falsehoods about their previous partners, some going so far as to fabricate accusations of sexual abuse, as a result alienating them from their children and destroying their reputations in the community. I worked with one client who was estranged from her father because her mother claimed he had been sexually inappropriate with her as a young child. It was only in adulthood that she became aware that her mother was a chronic liar and often embellished the "facts" to her own advantage. Eventually, the daughter reconciled with her father, but she had to mourn the loss of the relationship she might have enjoyed with him throughout her adolescence.

An example closer to home concerns my own post-divorce reactions to family celebrations. In the early years, when the situation was still acrimonious (or at the very least, tense), my former husband and I alternated attendance at holidays, birthdays, and graduations, or else kept a respectful distance to avoid putting our children in an untenable position. When it was his turn to host a holiday event, I became morose, harboring intense feelings of exclusion and conjuring images of my ex and children happily together while I was on the outside looking in with "my face pressed against the glass".

The situation changed after my daughter, who lived out of town, gave birth to our first grandchildren— twins, in fact. When she visited, I resented every minute without access to the adorable twins. On one important holiday when my daughter could only attend one family celebration, she would have had to choose between her parents. It occurred to me that if I invited my former husband (who, by this time, had remarried and had a daughter) to a celebration at my home, he might reciprocate in the future, and neither of us would be left out. I decided that my love for my children and grandchildren far outweighed my lingering resentment toward my former husband. In maintaining a distancing stance towards him, I was only hurting myself.

Since then, we have celebrated all family milestones and holidays together. Friends marvel at this arrangement, some considering me a saint for putting my children's feelings ahead of my own. They fail to understand that I did not do this only, or even primarily, for my children but for myself. I found it far less painful to be inclusive and enjoy my family than to be mired in a vengeful stance. The irony is that these initially forced interactions have allowed us to be less resentful of each other over time. There may be some truth to the notion that "you fake it until you make it". At family gatherings, my husband and I have enjoyed some pleasant conversations with my former husband and his wife. During a recent holiday weekend, I was amused to find myself making breakfast for both of my former and current husbands.

The main point I am making is that, in general, a healthy response to being wronged is to get on with our lives, using our energy constructively to form other relationships or to engage in productive career or leisure activities. In other words, the best revenge is living well.

In contrast to responding to wrongs with self-defeating behavior, others who have suffered loss or trauma may engage in a "survivor mission"[15]. They believe that they can transform the meaning of their personal tragedy by making it a basis for helping others. This coping mechanism is far less deleterious than exacting revenge because it has altruistic consequences. The problem, however, is that it interferes with the ability of hurt or traumatized individuals to entirely get on with their lives and put the past hurt, devastation, and betrayal behind them. In essence, the primary disadvantage of helping others with similar problems is to be reminded repeatedly of one's own hurt.

9

On hurt feelings

Some people seem predisposed to experiencing hurt feelings. Perhaps they were always temperamentally sensitive or they may have grown up in a family marked by criticism or disinterest, resulting in heightened vigilance to the slightest signs of rejection.

As a therapist, I encourage my clients to determine whether a rejection is actually occurring in their lives, or whether they are overreacting to the present in terms of their past experience. If appropriate, I also encourage them to check with the "offending" parties as to whether the presumed rejection is intended. This strategy can be particularly useful with family and friends; however, it is less appropriate in more formal relationships where such inquiries might imply insecurity and the need for excessive reassurance.

A more insidious source of feeling rejected is our tendency to attribute our own feelings to other people. If a given behavior on our part would signify rejection of the other, we might erroneously conclude that the same action directed towards us is, likewise, a sign of rejection.

An everyday occurrence that I have often experienced is a lukewarm response to one of my overtures, such as "I'll let you know," coupled with a failure to respond within a reasonable time. If I responded in this manner, it would be my way of politely trying to turn down the invitation, perhaps in the hope that a more appealing offer would materialize. Consequently, I am inclined to interpret such responses from others as ways of signaling disinterest in spending time with me. It took me years to realize that there were other explanations unrelated to rejection that could account for wishy-washy responses to such invitations. For example, one of my close friends recently admitted that she was prone to depression. As a result, she never knew until the last minute whether she would have enough energy to socialize.

This type of misunderstanding is particularly problematic for couples. In Gary Chapman's book, *The 5 Love Languages*, he proposes that couples express love in five distinct ways and that both partners may not share the same language of love[16]. A common example revolves around gift-giving. One member of the couple might be very thoughtful and considerate about choosing exactly the right gift for important occasions, whereas the partner may not view gifts as an expression of love. For a person who is inclined to purchase carefully considered gifts, the absence of a gift or a generic gift may feel like a lack of caring because they would judge their partner's behavior by what it would mean had they themselves chosen a comparable gift. This might be a serious misattribution because perhaps the partner might express love in countless other ways.

On a recent talk show, a caller described his financially-strapped girlfriend's response to receiving a $400 Walmart gift certificate from him. He was mystified about her hurt and anger because it was such an impersonal gift, one that was exactly what he would have wanted in comparable circumstances. Interestingly, participants in the talk show were evenly divided in their opinions, with most of the women regarding it as an insulting, impersonal gift, and most of the men applauding the man's actions. In long-standing relationships, it is important for members of a couple to understand that their primary way of expressing caring may differ from that of their partner.

I can recount an amusing personal example along these lines. Many years ago, a Valentine's Day gift of a smoked chicken from my former husband prompted an outburst of tears about the non-romantic nature of the gift. My ex, by contrast, regarded it as a considerate gesture. As a young family with very little time or money, he imagined that a ready-made meal would brighten my day. The reactions of our three children were interesting. My daughter, in her mid-teens at the time, thought it was a terrible gift and indicated that she would break up with her boyfriend immediately if he gave her a gift like that. My middle child commiserated with his father's good intentions and was equally baffled by my reaction. My youngest son (always the peace-keeper) thought the gift was stupid but that I didn't have to say so. His preferred course of action (for me) was pretending to like it.

I am also reminded of a friend who used to express profound disappointment in her husband's repeated failure to acknowledge her birthday. She gradually came to appreciate the many other ways in which he was loving and considerate and ultimately reconciled herself to never receiving a gift. Years later, I remarked on the beautiful earrings she was wearing on the occasion of her 30th anniversary and commented that her husband must have finally registered the message about the importance of gifts. She smiled wryly and indicated that her daughter, now a young adult, took her father shopping and insisted that he buy an appropriate present.

In summary, it is important to be aware that we often feel needlessly hurt because we make false attributions about present-day interactions from our past experience or equally false attributions from our own inner experience.

____

10

On why we worry

____

Some people are "born worriers". They worry indiscrimi-
nately about both important and trivial matters. Others
confine their worries to eventualities that have great significance for them. I have given some thought to the psychological functions served by what is often perceived as
needless worry. It seems to me that worrying allows us to
maintain an illusion of control in an otherwise unpredictable world.

Some people can be considered superstitious worriers.
They imagine that by worrying about a negative eventu-
ality in advance, they can magically guarantee its non-
occurrence. I frequently observed this phenomenon with
high school students who displayed excessive drama about
forthcoming exams. Somehow the biggest worriers
managed to obtain the best grades.

Other people worry to guard against disappointment.
By anticipating a negative outcome, they are hoping to
lessen the impact if it materializes. Unfortunately, this
strategy is counterproductive because instead of being
disappointed once by a negative outcome, continued

worrying makes them disappointed many times over. If the anticipated disappointment does not occur, then they have worried unnecessarily. Corrie ten Boom aptly expresses this sentiment: "worry does not empty tomorrow of its sorrow, it empties today of its strength"[16].

For others, worrying has the somewhat adaptive effect of problem-solving. They foresee a negative event and strategize about ways to minimize the possibility of its occurrence. As Winston Churchill stated, "let our advance worrying become advance thinking and planning". An everyday example relates to the vicissitudes of air travel. Some people are so concerned about missing an important event that they schedule their travels many days in advance.

I, for example, am much more disposed to worry and to manufacture so-called "adaptive solutions". When organizing my oldest son's bar mitzvah, the first major social event that I planned on my own, I was excessively concerned with the smallest details. After hearing horror stories of weddings ruined by bad weather, my "adaptive solution" was to insist on back-up gas stoves in case of a power failure. By most people's standards, this was extreme overkill or neurotic behavior. Nevertheless, it calmed my anxiety.

On the other hand, more lackadaisical types are less disappointed when their plans fail to materialize. One of my sons and his wife, who are committed non-worriers, made winter honeymoon plans that included a very tight flight connection. When they missed their connection, the newlyweds cheerfully and creatively generated alternate plans.

The central point is that worrying allows some of us to arrive at solutions that reduce the likelihood of disappointing outcomes. In fact, the entire insurance industry capitalizes upon people's worries, assuring clients that in the event of unforeseen disasters, the world will be restored to its original state. Nevertheless, many less anxious people consider it futile to worry about highly unlikely events. I have some friends who are downright allergic to this kind of "fretting," refusing to take out insurance policies and refusing to live their lives as if disaster will strike any minute, in contrast to others who plan carefully for all possible eventualities. By comparing these different approaches to thinking about the future, one can see that worrying is at its core an attempt to control unpredictable outcomes.

11

On sabotaging success

I have worked with many clients whose stated goal was to be successful, yet they repeatedly undercut their possibilities for achievement. I have come to understand that inhibition of success does not lend itself to any one dynamic formulation; several distinct patterns emerge. The therapeutic task is to help the client explore which of these dynamics, rooted in childhood, is responsible for their role in limiting the opportunities for success.

Sigmund Freud initially postulated that "success neurosis" originates in the child's anxiety and guilt about competing with and outdoing the same-sex parent[18]. Underlying this, the desire to romantically dispossess the same-sex parent is fraught with anxiety and guilt because the child also loves and needs that parent and, therefore, does not want to risk either hurting the parent or receiving parental retribution. Freud originally designated this phenomenon the *Oedipal complex*[18]. Because these fantasies are relinquished in childhood in most cases, they do not create difficulties in adult life. There are instances, however, where the opposite-sex parent is emotionally seductive (in fact preferring the child to their spouse) or the same-sex parent is particularly vulnerable or punitive. In these cases, the fears persist into adulthood, and the adult acts in such a way as to inhibit the dangerous success which is unconsciously seen as winning the Oedipal battle and therefore evoking parental retribution.

My work with university students provided ample opportunity to learn about the family constellations of students who were limiting their academic achievement because of concerns about being more successful than their parents. Typically, parents of such students were prevented by circumstances from obtaining a good education. Many were frustrated by unfulfilling jobs and low levels of material attainment. Academic success generated uneasiness because the students' opportunities would far outstrip those of their parents.

The prospect of success is particularly threatening when academic achievement is fostered by the opposite-sex parent. Female students with intellectual fathers who have turned to their daughters rather than their wives for intellectual fulfillment express uneasiness about getting close to their fathers through intellectual pursuits. I also observed a similar pattern in male students whose ambitious mothers denigrated their husbands' lack of success and pressured their sons to make up for their husbands' failures.

When I was a university student, I also had the opportunity to observe this dynamic at close hand. I was in awe of, and more than a little bit jealous of, the close relationship between one of my close friends and her father, who regularly scheduled "date nights" to discuss her literature courses. Her mother, who was a warm and lovely woman, was not intellectually inclined, so her father turned to his daughter for intellectual companionship. This long-term friend later confided that she eventually became aware of the negative impact of her father's emotional seductiveness when she observed her father's treatment of her own children.

Sibling rivalry can also inhibit later success. Most children have a deep wish to be the favorite child. If parents don't play favorites, these longings do not create difficulties in adult life because the fantasies are never actualized. However, there are families in which the parents clearly favor one child. The favorite child's response might be to limit success in childhood so that they won't stand out from their siblings and can sustain good relationships with them that are not tainted by envy. In adulthood, success is viewed as a finite commodity, as if one person's success will make for another's failure. At a deeper level, success is viewed as taking parental affection away from the siblings. The guilt and anxiety about these rivalrous feelings lead to the sabotage of successful endeavors.

Many years ago, I worked with a female client who felt guilty about her grades being superior to those of her classmates. When we examined the origins of her guilt, she recalled writing scholarship exams to enter high school and purposely giving the wrong answers so that her performance would not exceed that of her siblings. She was one of ten children in a family that did not value education, and she wanted to ensure that she did not stand out from her brothers and sisters.

Another dynamic that causes people to feel uneasy about success is fear of moving into another world and the feeling of loneliness generated by leaving behind those they know and love. I have often observed this response in children of immigrant families whose parents value their children's successes, which are regarded as a means of vindicating their own hardships, and at the same time feel threatened by those same achievements. These young adults report being the target of comments such as "who do you think you are?" and "now you think you are too good for us!" The unfortunate reality is that the children do move into a different world, which cannot include the parents, and the children and parents both feel a profound sense of loss.

Even if the parents' primary reaction is to feel pride in their children's accomplishments, these adult children continue to be tormented by the guilty self-reproach that they abandoned their parents. This feeling of guilt, as well as a sense of loss, may be manifested in a dampening down of their later successes.

Moreover, further emotional complications arise from the feeling that they do not fit in and are not really accepted in their new communities. It is as if they are caught between two worlds, not belonging to either one. I have known people from impoverished backgrounds who continued to dress and act in a way that understated their wealth even after attaining considerable financial success. Their discomfort about leaving their original community behind motivated them to continue to accentuate their similarities to those with whom they grew up.

A client recently recounted her experience of being accepted, on scholarship, into a special school for gifted children. The majority of the students in the new school were from a higher social class, and she felt very different from them. At the same time, her siblings and neighborhood friends expressed resentment at her being singled out for special schooling. This resulted in feelings of alienation from her old and new peers, prompting her to adopt a life-long pattern of accommodation to gain acceptance.

Several literary works have themes that revolve around the painful emotions generated by extreme upward mobility. "The Glass Castle" by Jeanette Walls, "Hillbilly Elegy" by J.D. Vance, and "Educated" by Tara Westover are memoirs in which the authors describe mixed feelings about escaping their impoverished circumstances and the painful awareness of not belonging to the more affluent world into which they have been catapulted by means of their education[19, 20, 21]. In all of these books, the authors describe how they continue to be burdened by the demons of their chaotic family histories.

Another dynamic that can sabotage success is a disguised expression of aggression. Students who act in such a way seem to be driven to fail as a vengeful act towards parents who have exploited them for narcissistic purposes. Characteristically, these families place extraordinary emphasis on their children's achievements, which they view as conferring status on the family. There are two deleterious consequences of this behavior. Firstly, the children feel that their autonomy is threatened by their parents, who have co-opted their successes for themselves. Secondly, they feel they are not valued as people in their own right, but only insofar as their accomplishments can aggrandize their parents. These students purposely fail as a way of disappointing their parents, thereby depriving them of the pride they would have had in their children's success.

Finally, what appears to be an inhibition of success may be a fear of failure. By procrastinating and not giving their full effort, a student can tell themself that if they fail, it can be attributed to the fact that they did not "really try," a phenomenon known as *self-handicapping*[22]. The term was first introduced by Edward Jones, whereby the limiting of opportunity for success by insufficient effort allows individuals to protect their self-esteem from feelings of inadequacy engendered by possible failure. The unfortunate consequence is that they have no opportunity to derive genuine self-esteem from the successes they might have attained if they had put forth their best effort. Ironically, the strategy of self-handicapping, which is designed to protect self-esteem, has the opposite consequence, limiting the opportunity to enhance self-confidence.

12

On commitment phobias

A number of my female clients dated men who were unable to commit to a relationship. These men abruptly ended the relationship when the women perceived it to be going particularly well. In some cases, the men did not disappear altogether, engaging instead in a repeated pattern of distancing, attempting to re-establish the relationship, and further distancing. I've also worked with commitment-phobic men who profess to want a relationship but find fault with every woman. Only when the pattern recurs with many women do the men identify it as a problem and seek therapeutic help. It is important to note that both men and women can be commitment-phobic. However, in my clinical experience, the majority of commitment-phobes have been men, and the examples I give here reflect that.

I've given a lot of thought to the dynamic underpinnings of commitment phobia. There are a number of interrelated causes that can be traced back to early, problematic mother-son relationships.

In some cases, the commitment-phobes seem to have

intense fears of abandonment or enmeshment originating in childhood. These feelings become intensified with increasing intimacy in adult relationships, resulting in subsequent distancing. With sufficient distance, however, the anxiety diminishes, increasing their comfort with re-establishing contact. This dynamic can account for the characteristic push/pull nature of these relationships.

A related possibility is that these men behave towards important women in their adult lives much like significant figures behaved towards them in childhood. Essentially, they actively do to others what they passively endured as children. Men who have been repeatedly abandoned by their mothers may act out the same pattern with their adult lovers, unconsciously expressing the anger suppressed in their youth by displacing their revenge onto the wrong people. It is as if they have a profound, probably unconscious, need to betray others to assuage their deep-seated feelings of abandonment and betrayal.

Another determinant involves low self-esteem and intense need for validation from multiple women. Such men typically enjoy the challenge and narcissistic glow of arousing interest in a new woman. After the conquest, however, they still feel empty, so they repeat the pattern with new women to receive a fresh dose of validation. As children, these men never attained love or approval from their parents, which interfered with the internalization of feelings of self-worth. Repeated attempts to seek external validation in adulthood do not fill the inner emptiness created by the original lack of approval. If children experience more optimal parenting, they can internalize parental love and approval, which is reflected in genuine self-worth and less need for validation from others. Heinz Kohut has written extensively about the importance of early mirroring in developing genuine self-esteem that does not depend on external sources of approval[23].

My personal interest in the dynamics underlying commitment phobias was prompted by my first experience of post-divorce dating. Although the man in question had many superficially desirable characteristics (including being attractive and a good conversationalist), I noticed that whenever the prospect of real intimacy arose, he would inform me that he was spending time with other women who were "just friends". Shortly after making tentative vacation plans with me, he finalized similar travel arrangements with his brother. He also flirted shamelessly with waitresses and retail clerks in a way that made me feel invisible. In addition, he made me feel self-conscious about what I regarded as minor flaws in my appearance. Because of my vulnerability at that time and the lack of comparable experiences in the past, it took me several months to realize how this toxic interaction was eroding my precarious self-esteem.

There were many red flags that I missed. For example, he had previously dated many lovely women, some of whom I knew, and he had found flaws in all of them. Ironically, many of those women found happiness in subsequent long-term relationships, whereas he continued to bounce from one short-term relationship to another. The extremely close relationships that he maintained with his adult children and a wide circle of friends had led me to believe that he could maintain a close relationship with a romantic partner. I have since come to realize that many commitment-phobic men can maintain excellent relationships with their friends and children. Their anxieties about intimacy seem to be evoked only in relationships with romantic partners, resulting in the characteristic push/pull pattern. Long after I remarried, I ran into some of his friends who mentioned their inclination to forewarn me about his inability to make a commitment. They had initially remained silent out of loyalty to him, but they were nevertheless pleased that I eventually "saw the light" and ended the relationship.

When women enter therapy because they are involved with commitment-phobic men, they typically feel anxious, confused, and filled with self-recrimination. The therapeutic work helps them appreciate the dynamics of their partners, which allows them to stop blaming themselves. They also become more cognizant of the push/pull nature of their relationships. Eventually, they understand that the only predictable aspect of their relationships is unpredictability because commitment-phobes cannot commit to staying or to leaving. This awareness may empower them to end these unfulfilling relationships because they are ready to abandon the hope that "this time will be different".

Therapy also focuses on early red flags that the client failed to notice. For example, commitment-phobes are likely to have broken up repeatedly with past partners. Moreover, they tend to establish rigid boundaries early on, keeping their girlfriends apart from friends and family, as if preparing for the eventual dissolution of the relationship. Awareness of these early red flags allows people to be appropriately cautious in subsequent dating.

Men who enter therapy for commitment issues are much more difficult to help than women are. First, they are often unaware of the problem until they have repeated the pattern many times. Moreover, their fear of intimacy and anger about abandonment may be deep-seated. To complicate matters further, they may have trouble committing to the therapy in the same way that they have difficulty committing to other relationships. As a result, I have often been unable to get beyond having these clients recognize their dynamics. This awareness at least allows them to take responsibility for their behavior so that they can stop misleading women about their emotional availability for long-term relationships.

13

On three chances for a family

Clients often seek therapy because they have had traumatic or non-nurturing childhoods. The primary therapeutic task is to help them mourn what they did not receive and, sadly, what can never be replaced. Equally important is to help them attain what is possible in their life by making them aware that the family we are born into is only our first chance for a warm family experience. As adults, we can create new families by partnering and having children. When we partner with someone, moreover, we can derive enjoyment from our partner's family. However, some people are so embittered by their harsh childhood circumstances that they deprive themselves of subsequent family experiences.

When we choose to have our own children, we can experience vicarious gratification from their childhood by providing the love and protection that we did not receive. Unfortunately, it is also possible to behave towards our children in the same dysfunctional manner that our parents behaved towards us. In fact, some people choose not to have children out of fear of behaving like their parents did.

When we become attached to someone, we have opportunities for enjoying our partners' families. I have known people who rejected their partners' families, and others who actively sought partners with warm, accepting families. One of my clients was estranged from both of her divorced parents and chose a boyfriend largely because of being enthralled with his parents and siblings. She spent important holidays with her boyfriend's family rather than her own despite considerable guilt about rejecting her own family. Eventually she realized that she loved her boyfriend's family more than the boyfriend himself and severed the relationship. As a result, she had to endure the very painful loss of her boyfriend's family to whom she had become intensely attached.

I have also known several women whose mothers passed away when they were adolescents. In some cases, they embraced their husbands' families, particularly their mothers-in-law, feeling that these relationships truly enriched their lives. In other cases, their husbands' warm families reminded them of their feelings of loss, which led to distancing and the avoidance of family visits, thereby depriving themselves of new family experiences. Their reactions may have been influenced by the envy dynamic described previously whereby they avoided or denigrated experiences that might stir up painful feelings of envy.

I observed a similar reaction in a male client whose childhood family structure was very unusual. In adulthood, he became somewhat estranged from his mother, who entered into a religious community and whose contact with him was very limited. When he eventually married and had children, he anticipated enjoying holidays and birthdays with his wife's much more typical extended family. He also looked forward to vicarious enjoyment of his children's interactions with grandparents and cousins.

In therapy, however, he recounted that these gatherings made him feel extremely depressed. Not only did they bring him into contact with his childhood longings for a normal family and his original feelings of deprivation, but he also became aware of the degree of current estrangement from his own mother from observations of his wife's comfortable interactions with her mother. Instead of attempting to integrate himself into her family, he tended to withdraw, depriving himself of the enriching family experiences that his in-laws might have provided.

14

On social media

In recent years, my clients' impetus to seek therapy was often provided by their engagement with social media. Therapeutic work revolved around painful feelings of rejection, betrayal, envy, exclusion, and defectiveness.

In the pre-social media environment, if a couple severed a long-standing relationship, neither partner had any way of knowing how the other was faring without resorting to stalking or plying mutual friends for information, both being unsavory and potentially ruinous alternatives. It was difficult enough without social media to manage the understandable feelings of rejection, betrayal, and abandonment without harboring fantasies that our ex-partners were faring much better than we were and that they were moving on without experiencing painful consequences of the breakup. In the absence of actual evidence, our imaginations had free rein.

Now that it is fashionable to post status updates and photos of our daily activities on social media, we have a window, however imperfect, on our former partners' social engagements and love interests. This information can be painful in various respects. Most damaging are the intense feelings of jealousy about our former partners' romantic interests and rich social lives. Moreover, that "information" devalues the former relationship if we perceive our former partners as capable of getting into high social gear while we wallow in sorrow. One client recently sought therapy after observing on Facebook that his former lover was not only dating someone else but was also enthusiastically engaging in previously unshared activities while he continued to languish at home.

Social media can trigger feelings of rejection in a multitude of ways. A very shy client sought therapy when a male high school friend rejected her Facebook friend request after they moved to different cities for their university studies. She was devastated to learn that he had accepted the friend requests of others. Because of her secret romantic feelings for him, she was doubly hurt by the realization that her feelings were not reciprocated and that he was even adverse to superficial contact with her.

Photos posted on social media reveal our exclusion from social engagements involving peers or relatives. Aside from the obvious feeling of exclusion, these situations can also generate jealousy and a sense of unworthiness. These feelings can even be provoked by postings by relative strangers. Quintessential photos of happy family gatherings can make us feel that everyone else is joyful and connected while we are deeply flawed in our failure to have similar support systems. Some people have comparable reactions to holiday cards that depict happy families and their pets. Envious feelings are all the more intense when we are bombarded with pictures of people enjoying seemingly unattainable but deeply longed-for relationships. These reactions can arise when single people view wedding pictures, infertile couples view photos of adorable babies, and seniors without grandchildren observe pictures of their friends' grandchildren.

Social media can stir up painful feelings not only in internet-obsessed adolescents and young adults but in people of any age. Recently, I met with a woman in her seventies whose health had prevented her and her husband from making their customary winter sojourn. She was extremely hurt by Facebook photos of her daughter's family socializing with her sister's family while she was left out in the cold, both literally and figuratively. Not only did she feel excluded from the seemingly happy get-together, but she experienced feelings of betrayal by her daughter for socializing with her sister, towards whom she harbored ambivalent feelings.

One of the strategies adopted by some people to avoid such painful feelings is to remove themselves from all social media platforms. This creates an especially difficult situation for young people because of the many invitations that are issued exclusively on social media. For them, abandoning social media is accompanied by a realistic fear of missing out (FOMO).

PART III

Relationship Dynamics

15

On toxic relationships

The signature indication of a toxic relationship is that it leaves us feeling diminished and depleted, whereas a healthy relationship allows us to feel replenished, energized, and valued.

Two subtle determinants of toxic relationships merit clarification. One revolves around the mechanism of *projective identification*, a term introduced by Bion and further elaborated upon by Ogden[24]. Simply put, this refers to the transfer of negative feelings from one person to another, resulting in the second person expressing the feelings of the first, who can then disavow their own uncomfortable emotions. For this to occur, the toxic person must behave in a manner that makes the recipient feel the way they do.

For example, a person with intense feelings of inadequacy might subject us to a barrage of criticism until we start to feel inadequate ourselves. Accordingly, they have succeeded in transferring their feelings of inadequacy such that they no longer have to be in touch with their own uncomfortable feelings. At the bridge table, I often notice that the most insecure individuals roll their eyes at their partners' mistakes. Their partners end up feeling stupid and the eye-rollers don't have to acknowledge their own feelings of intellectual inferiority.

This mechanism of projective identification can be invoked for any uncomfortable emotion. A classic example is of a family whose members happily engage with one another until the agitated father arrives, yells at everyone, and suddenly the entire family is fighting. The father has successfully transferred his feelings of anger and anxiety onto his family members while he has magically calmed down.

Another example is of men who are deeply ashamed of their own sexuality and criticize their partners' enthusiasm for sex, making their partners feel as ashamed as they do. Some people are particular ink blots for the projected feelings of others, absorbing and expressing them with unusual intensity. Successful therapy would facilitate recognition of these toxic interactions so that the client can repudiate and disown these negative emotions.

A second and less obvious reason why a relationship might feel toxic is if one of the participants harbors deep envy of the other. In that case, the envied person, who might be the target of direct and oblique criticism, ends up feeling demeaned without necessarily being aware of the envy of the other. In fact, feeling criticized is one of the hallmarks of a toxic relationship. Regardless of the origin of the criticism (projective identification of inadequacy or envy), our natural response to criticism is to defensively justify our behavior.

In my experience, the best way to handle destructive criticism is to directly address the *process* of criticism rather than its *content*. If we respond directly to the content as if it warrants a response, we are lending credibility to that criticism. A more effective strategy is to expose the toxicity of the other person by highlighting the critical process, exposing the negative intent behind the criticism. Often this results in embarrassment or, at the very least, shuts down the negative interaction.

A striking example occurred at the bridge club when I was a novice player. An experienced older player expressed surprise at my elementary mistakes, given that I was sufficiently intelligent to obtain a PhD. My initial inclination was to justify my mistake by explaining my faulty thinking. In other words, I addressed the content of the criticism. To my delight, however, I recouped by pointing out the process of being criticized. Specifically, I questioned why he, as an experienced player, needed to put down a novice. I pointed out that a more productive approach would have been to help me become a better player by pointing out my mistakes rather than by making me feel stupid. He was taken aback but subsequently behaved in a very constructive fashion. By pointing out the process of the criticism, I had challenged him to examine the motive behind his critical demeanor. In short, it is more effective to respond to direct or implied criticism by confronting the person with their critical stance rather than derailing the conversation by responding to the critical content.

In another example, one of my clients described how upset she was by her mother-in-law's perpetual criticism of her homemaking abilities. Her first, entirely ineffective response was to justify why she chose to do things in the way she did. I encouraged her to address the process by challenging her mother-in-law's tendency to criticize. By exposing her mother-in-law's penchant for criticism, she was able to end the cycle of negative interactions.

In general, therapeutic work helps clients to recognize the feeling of being criticized (often criticisms are veiled) and to adopt effective responses such as addressing the process rather than the content.

16

On severing ties with families

Several clients have questioned their justification in severing all communication with their families. Therapy is not a value-free endeavor. Therapists who do not hold strong convictions about family values may inadvertently encourage their clients to sever ties with family members when those relationships cause distress.

I knew one analyst who had experienced a divorce, and eventually, every one of his clients divorced as well. The analyst's values regarding marriage may have guided the direction of his therapy such that he influenced his clients to leave their relationships rather than expending effort to resolve the problems. By contrast, I encourage my clients to attempt to salvage relationships with family members whenever possible. My emphasis is on appreciating the redeeming aspects of the relationships while becoming less intensely triggered by the toxic aspects.

The therapist's role is not to foster love or hate of one's parents. Instead, the goal is to help clients maintain their self-esteem in the face of negative interactions. Doing so may necessitate some observational distance as a way of avoiding feelings of devastation from each instance of a parent's empathic failure.

Although it is normal as children to idealize our parents and take their word as gospel, adults can develop a more realistic appreciation of parents as human beings with their own challenges and limitations. If clients can be guided to view parental failures empathically as reflecting the parents' dynamics rather than their own failings, they may be able to interact with their parents without experiencing continuing assaults on their own self-worth.

This brings us to the issue of narcissistic parents who often put their own needs above those of their children. I recently worked with an adult client who was deeply hurt by her father's expectation, shortly after her mother's death, that she would want to spend time with his new girlfriend. She was furious at her father's lack of empathy for her grief. Therapy focused on her recognition of her father's narcissism, which had been expressed in many ways long before her mother's death, but from which she had been shielded by her loving mother. Our therapy also brought her into contact with the more caring parts of her father. Eventually, she was able to accept her father as he was rather than as she wanted him to be. As her expectations decreased, she could have more positive, if somewhat limited, interactions with him.

The important point is that her father was a *non-malignant narcissist*[25]. His self-centeredness functioned to raise his self-esteem, but it had the unintended consequence of a serious lack of empathy for his daughter.

By contrast, there are *malignant narcissists*[25]. Eric Fromm, who first coined this term, described the condition as "the most severe pathology and the root of the most vicious destructiveness and inhumanity"[25]. Later, Otto Kernberg noted that malignant narcissism goes beyond grandiosity to include sadistic elements, antisocial traits, lack of morality, and a need for power[26, 27]. Because malignant narcissists dehumanize the people with whom they associate, their relationships are truly toxic. Clients with family members who display these qualities would be well advised to break off all ties to avoid being the target of evil intent.

17

On the many facets of abuse

In the most severely abusive relationships, the primary emotions keeping victims bound to their abusers is fear. The abusers have often destroyed their victims' self-esteem and alienated them from family and friends. The victims may feel that they deserve the abuse and, in any event, they feel alone in the world with no one to turn to.

However, there are other equally abusive relationships in which the victims derive some gratification, possibly unconscious, from the relationships. I have known abusive individuals to react with extreme guilt after the abuse, showering their partners with deeply longed-for affection. It is almost as if their partners are willing to put up with the abuse so that they can bask in the affection that inevitably follows.

In other scenarios, we may know that a relationship is toxic and somewhat abusive, but we consciously stay in the relationship because the rewards outweigh the negative aspects. I have noticed this repeatedly at the bridge club. At times, I have chosen to put up with a nasty bridge partner in the hope that playing with a particularly accomplished bridge player would improve my game.

Outside observers often challenge the person who is seemingly abused— in bridge as in life— as to why they tolerate such a nasty person. What the observer does not always understand is that the good sometimes outweighs the bad and the so-called victims do not feel utterly powerless. The main point is that there is a crucial distinction between situations in which people cannot escape from their abusers because of their terror, lack of power, or neediness, and those who make an empowered decision to engage in seemingly toxic relationships because they value aspects of those relationships.

18

On managing conflict: optimal ways of communication

Most people in intimate relationships fight from time to time. The important point is not whether we fight, but how we fight. A prevalent theme underlying conflict, especially in couples, is resentment at not having our needs met. Our tendency is to attack the other for not doing or saying the right thing. The problem with lashing out in this manner is that our partners become angry and defensive. Because they are so focused on protecting themselves from the attack, they fail to attend to the legitimacy of the complaint.

A more effective strategy is to say what we need and express our hurt feelings directly. This is what John Gottman, a psychologist who has studied marriage extensively, refers to as the use of "I" statements rather than "you" statements[28]. "I" statements reflect our own feelings, perceptions, and experiences, while "you" statements attack the other. Furthermore, "I" statements not only allow our partners to understand our unmet needs, but of equal importance, they generate empathy for our feelings, which may be a powerful motivator for change.

One of the primary reasons that we attack the other rather than directly expressing what we need is that we magically think that those closest to us should know what we need without explicit directives. The reality is that the only recipients of that kind of empathy are infants, and even that is limited. There is a wonderful poem by Robert Frost, "Revelation," which speaks to this theme, concluding "But so with all, from babes that play / At hide-and-seek to G-d afar, / So all who hide too well away / Must speak and tell us where they are"[29].

Another effective strategy for communicating our feelings of dissatisfaction is what the Urban Dictionary calls the *shit sandwich*[30]. A shit sandwich "is designed to make bad news, advice, or rejection more palatable" for the recipient[30]. The trick is to begin by expressing appreciation for the other, then expressing discontent, and then concluding on a more positive note that emphasizes the good aspects of the relationship. This approach allows the target of the complaint to feel less attacked and correspondingly less defensive. It also makes the other person feel appreciated rather than a total disappointment.

Both of these strategies ("I" statements and the shit sandwich) are also effective in more impersonal contexts. I have noticed in conversations with airline personnel, car dealers, and service providers that I am much more likely to be fairly compensated if I use "I" statements, resist attacking, and acknowledge the helpful aspects of the interaction.

A recent conversation with good friends provides an instructive example. My husband and I were exchanging stories with these friends about some of the challenges of travel. Both men admitted that when situations arose where they felt entitled to compensation, they often asked their wives to speak to the appropriate parties. They described becoming impatient and antagonistic and ultimately unsuccessful in their attempts to obtain remuneration.

Our friends then recounted a recent incident where they had booked a hotel over the internet with a non-refundable room rate (i.e., no cancellations of changes). The following day, they noticed a substantial price reduction on the website. The husband's call to the hotel resulted in an altercation with the hotel clerk, who was entirely unsympathetic to his plight. I suggested that, upon arrival at the hotel, instead of lambasting a clerk for the hotel's "idiotic" policies (a "you" statement), that they calmly explain their situation and state "our" misfortune in having booked the hotel before the rate reduction (an "I" statement). I also suggested that while registering their dissatisfaction, they could express their appreciation for the excellent service they had experienced during previous stays at the hotel (shit sandwich). This less attacking, more appreciative approach resulted in an upgrade in accommodations as well as a substantial rate reduction.

On the importance of a
common value system

After many years of observing relationships in my personal and professional life, I have concluded that three ingredients seem essential for lasting relationships. The first two, genuine friendship and chemistry, are intuitively obvious. However, the death knell for many relationships is the absence of a third and less obvious ingredient, which is a common value system or worldview. A common worldview affects our attitudes towards money, time, parenting, religion, and even politics. If a couple shares a common value system, they largely agree about the really important things. In the absence of a common worldview, the potential for arguments is limitless.

Even if we are largely in sync with our partners, there are invariably residual areas of disagreement. In these instances, it is important to be able to negotiate and compromise. This might mean taking turns getting one's own way or meeting somewhere in the middle. In my experience, the partner who feels most intensely about a specific issue is the one who receives the ultimate deference on that issue. If we care about our partners' feelings as much as we care about our own, it is much easier to compromise.

A common value system also makes it more likely that our partners will value in us what we appreciate in ourselves. This is important for us to feel really known. An illustrative example is a beautiful woman who values her intellect but whose partner does not view intelligence as an important attribute in a partner. In this situation, she would not feel fully seen or appreciated for her whole self.

In choosing a partner, we often focus on common interests without considering whether we also share a common worldview. We can usually find people other than our partners to share our interests, but sharing a life meaningfully requires someone who also shares our values. Relationships based on common interests that are not accompanied by a common value system are doomed to fail in one way or another.

In certain instances, a divergence in values may cause severe damage to the relationship. This occurs when accommodating our partners does not allow us to remain true to our own core values. To do so makes us feel as though we are "selling our souls" and evokes profound resentment. In these cases, it is probably best to prioritize our own values.

The following example provides a cautionary tale. I knew someone whose wife objected to his contact with his somewhat limited brother for whom he felt considerable responsibility. She went so far as to forbid him to invite his brother to their house. All attempts to generate empathy for his brother fell on deaf ears. The man did not choose to leave the marriage because he and his wife had children. Instead he saw his brother surreptitiously, becoming increasingly resentful towards his wife. Although this marriage was not terminated, it was permanently damaged from an emotional standpoint.

A common worldview is also important in non-romantic friendships and in family relationships. We tend to feel closest to, and have less conflict with, those who share our value systems. These are the people who make us feel appreciated and truly known.

20

On why can't we still be friends

Individuals who terminate a long-term, intimate relationship often express the wish to remain "friends" with their exes, who they view as a "best friend". In my experience, this is almost impossible, unless the decision is truly mutual and both people no longer harbor romantic or sexual feelings for the other. Jealousy is a corollary of romantic love. If either partner gets involved in a new relationship, jealous feelings are evoked, and the other finds it extremely painful to hear about the former partner's new love interest.

The wish to remain friends may be motivated by an attempt to forestall feelings of intense grief over the rupture of a long-term relationship. However, turning to the person who is the source of the pain doesn't work because the same person cannot be part of the problem as well as part of the solution.

Inevitably, after initial attempts to remain friends, one party realizes that it is too difficult and decides to break off all contact. At that point, the sadness about the severed relationship is most intensely felt. Should clients seek help at this juncture, the role of the therapist is to help them truly mourn the loss of the relationship. It is important that they come into contact with their extreme feelings of sadness, which have been held at bay by remaining friends. It is equally important for them to become aware of the inevitable anger generated by feeling rejected and abandoned. Finally, it is necessary that they view their former partners more realistically. Often, the initial inclination is to idealize their partners and devalue themselves, blaming themselves for the failure of the relationship. The therapist can help them develop a more realistic appreciation of their own strengths and weaknesses as well as those of their former partners.

In general, it is also helpful for clients to recognize that some relationships may have been enriching despite their eventual dissolution. Often, a relationship allows us to learn some very important things about ourselves. At the very least, we also learn what qualities to look for in subsequent partners.

21

On offering advice to adult children

There are people who cannot resist giving advice to their friends and family. This tendency gets them into trouble because the recipients often feel that they are being criticized and resent unsolicited advice. I have developed several guidelines or "rules" for determining when it is appropriate to offer an opinion to adult children in particular.

The most important consideration is whether the topic at hand is truly of my concern. Suppose an adult child confides that they are making a financial investment which I consider unwise. If they are asking me to provide money, then, clearly, I have a right to express my opinion; otherwise, it is really not my business. If I am asked directly for my opinion, then it is obviously appropriate to give advice.

The first two considerations may be overridden by the importance of the topic under discussion. If health or safety might be compromised, then it is appropriate to offer advice that is neither solicited nor my concern. In such cases, it would be unethical not to make the person aware of potentially dangerous consequences.

Following these "rules" is not as clear-cut as it might seem, especially when we are very familiar with those to whom we are inclined to give advice. There are countless situations where I've had to bite my tongue when I disapprove of my children's decisions. On other occasions, in spite of my resolve to follow my own guidelines, I blurted out my unsolicited opinions. As parents of adult children, it is often difficult to remember that they are every bit as capable as we are of acquiring the necessary information to make intelligent decisions. I remember annoyance at my own mother for calling to remind me that my children should be dressed appropriately for the cold weather. Recently, I found myself apologizing before asking one of my sons if he remembered to transfer the insurance for his new car.

At times, when my family becomes annoyed at what they consider unnecessary meddling, I remind them that they should be happy to have a mother who displays concern. The problem is that although the advice-givers interpret their comments as expressions of caring, the recipients experience them as criticism or intrusiveness.

An additional dilemma arises about decisions regarding what is important enough to justify unsolicited advice. The answer is obviously subjective. What I consider critical may be inconsequential to my family. I have observed, however, that my point of view is more likely to be heard if I tactfully inquire whether they had considered the ramifications of a particular decision rather than bulldozing them with my opinions about what they should or should not do. On occasion, I have heard their vehement objections to my point of view on an issue, observing subsequently that my view had affected their final decision.

One example comes from one of my clients who sought help because of conflict with her adult children. In therapy, she became aware that she often offered unsolicited advice, which antagonized her children. On one occasion, she was asked to look after her grandchildren while the parents vacationed. She criticized their decision to vacation without the children, deeming them selfish. I pointed out that her only concern was whether or not to accede to their request of looking after the grandchildren in their absence. It was not her place to opine on including the children in their vacation plans or to pass judgment on their decision when they had not requested her opinion.

I have used similar guidelines when deciding whether to offer advice to a client. In therapy, a request for advice can be considered a request for clarification. As therapists, our role is to help clients articulate their own mixed feelings so that they can become aware of the relevant factors, weighing those factors out before making their own decisions. I would offer advice, of course, if a client was about to engage in dangerous or self-sabotaging behavior. In such cases, I suspend my therapeutic stance and offer a direct opinion.

22

On internet dating

The most opportune time to meet potential life-partners is when circumstances allow us to encounter a variety of people of similar age and like-mindedness. University (and for earlier generations, high school) provides such fertile meeting grounds. In more traditional, less mobile societies, couples also meet at church or are introduced by members of the community.

With young people increasingly delaying marriage and family in favor of educational and career opportunities, long-term relationships often have low priority in university despite providing an appropriate, perhaps optimal, context. In fact, many students believe that committed relationships at university would interfere with their academic focus and professional development.

Several of my clients expressed their preference for platonic or casual sexual relationships while at university. After graduation and subsequent relocation to optimize career opportunities, they became aware of the difficulty of meeting anyone other than work colleagues, who may be off-limits because of workplace rules. These and other factors have contributed to the increasing popularity of internet dating.

In my personal and professional life, I have encountered several people who succeeded in finding a suitable life partner on the Internet. However, some of my clients were so devastated by their internet dating experience that they abandoned the medium, sometimes after a single negative experience. It seems to me that the individuals who find internet dating most difficult are those who are exquisitely sensitive to rejection. I have repeatedly had to explain to clients that the failure of an initial meeting to generate a subsequent date cannot be interpreted as rejection. The choice of whether or not to pursue such a relationship is based on rapid, superficial evaluation by a total stranger, which is altogether different from rejection of one's deepest self.

For some people, however, the most minor rebuff is experienced as confirmation of their inherent unlovability, sending them into a tailspin from which it is difficult to recover. Interestingly, such rejection-sensitive individuals have great difficulty turning down a request for a second meeting when they are the ones who are uninterested in pursuing the relationship in the first place. Their challenge with rejecting others stems from their attribution that the other person will experience the rejection as painfully as they do.

Those who are most successful at internet dating have fundamentally good self-esteem and can maintain light-heartedness and humor about a brief meeting of two strangers to evaluate their potential for a long-term relationship. It has much in common with the mini-interviews at job fairs, where employers use first impressions to narrow down the field of job seekers. Presumably, individuals who are comfortable with speed-dating, perhaps the ultimate in superficiality, would be prime candidates for internet dating.

Desperation to find a partner can lead to over-sharing, resulting in pseudo-intimacy rather than genuine intimacy. Trust must be earned over an extended period of time as two people gradually get to know one another. Over-sharers experience intense embarrassment about having confided in someone who is uninterested in pursuing a relationship with them.

In short, internet dating is most effective for those who have basically good self-esteem and whose previous failure to find a partner stems from life circumstances or lack of motivation. By contrast, it is least effective and most prob-lematic for those whose chronic low self-esteem has prevented them from successfully engaging in romantic relationships.

On Life Cycle
Concerns

23

On life cycle concerns

In his writings, Erik Erikson describes the eight stages of psychosocial development from infancy to late adulthood[31]. The problems that I have observed over the course of fifty years as a therapist correspond in many ways to his final four stages. According to Erikson, the developmental task in the late teens and early 20s is achieving a sense of identity and the ego quality of fidelity, "an emotional awareness of who we are and the ability to sustain loyalties really pledged in spite of the inevitable contradictions and confusions of value systems"[32]. He contends that adolescents must consolidate their identity with respect to occupation, gender roles and, in some cultures, politics and religion.

Erikson describes the next stage as the ability to achieve intimacy, characterized by readiness to make long-term commitments to others. At this stage, people develop the capacity to forge reciprocal relationships along with the sacrifices and compromises entailed by such relationships. Avoidance of intimacy can lead to isolation and loneliness.

Middle-aged adults struggle with generativity, the ability to guide the next generation and contribute to society rather than stagnation. Generativity has broad applicability to family, work, and society. Contributions at that stage of life provide a sense of productivity and accomplishment. By contrast, stagnation implies a lack of productivity and purpose and a sense of meaninglessness.

Erikson designates *ego integrity versus despair* as the eighth and final stage, defining ego integrity as the ability to look back on life with "a sense of coherence and wholeness" and the satisfaction of a life well lived[33]. By contrast, despair results from feelings of failure at most developmental tasks, most notably the ability to sustain relationships and make productive and meaningful contributions to society.

I have had the opportunity to work with clients from 17 to 90 years of age. Although all of us struggle with the same fundamental emotions regardless of age, the content of our concerns varies markedly at different stages of the life cycle.

Problems presented by young adults during my time working at the McGill University Mental Health Service included broken love relationships, stress about academic performance with underlying fears of failure or uneasiness about success, difficulty individuating from overbearing and overprotective parents, absence of clear-cut goals after graduating from university, confusion about gender identity and, less commonly, guilt and shame about abandoning mentally ill parents to pursue their own lives.

For those entering therapy in their 30s and 40s, problematic relationships are the primary focus. Many men and women in committed partnerships have difficulty making their needs known to their partners. A significant issue is whether to remain in a disappointing relationship or to seek a more satisfying relationship despite the expected financial and emotional ramifications of such a disruption.

New parents who have experienced conflictual relationships with their own parents want to be more nurtu-
rant and less overbearing than their own parents, but they
have a persistent fear of repeating the dysfunctional
patterns that they experienced as children.

A particular challenge are the single men and women
who seek therapy because of difficulty finding, or
remaining in, long-term partnerships. The single men are
often commitment-phobes who express intense interest in
having a relationship. Nevertheless, they find fault with
every potential partner because of deep fears about intimacy originating in problematic mother-son relationships.
Some of the single women present with low self-esteem
and are somewhat phobic about men, which prevents them
from enjoying a romantic relationship. Other women were
in long-standing relationships in their teens or early 20s,
which eventually ended. Now that they are in their 30s,
they find it extremely difficult to meet appropriate partners
in a diminishing sample of single men. Some women,
nearing 40, are determined to have a child on their own,
but they struggle with guilt about not providing the child
with a father and with anxiety about the financial and
emotional aspects of raising a child single handedly.

Clients in their 50s, many of whom are "empty
nesters," often seek help in response to their children
leaving home. Those who have focused intensely on family
life question the possibility of resuming a quality relationship with their mate. Women whose primary identity once
revolved around raising a family often find it difficult to
relinquish their central role in the lives of their adult children. At the same time, middle-aged adults may experience some degree of role reversal relative to their own
parents who are facing declining health. Additionally,
career-oriented men and women may evaluate the degree

to which their work has been productive and meaningful. Therapeutic discussions with this age group focus primarily on overcoming a sense of purposelessness and meaninglessness. Practical aspects revolve around promoting their creative use of leisure time, whether by developing rewarding hobbies, pastimes, or volunteer work.

Seniors present with an entirely different set of problems. Clients in their 70s and 80s often have concerns that stem from the sacrifices and demands of caring for a sick partner. Because of devoting so much time and energy to their partners' needs at the expense of their own gratification, these clients become increasingly resentful about their own unmet needs. Although they are aware of becoming increasingly depressed and depleted, they are often unaware of their underlying resentment. Therapeutic work focuses on normalizing such feelings of resentment and giving them permission to be "selfish" enough to allow themselves to engage in some pleasurable activities on their own and take a reprieve from the caretaker role.

Seniors who best deal with these issues are those who were never "compulsive care-givers"[34]. David Malan describes a dynamic whereby some people, deprived of a nurturing childhood, compulsively give to others as a way of denying awareness of their own dependency needs and also as a way of denying resentment of their unmet childhood needs[35]. When confronted in later life with realistic circumstances that demand caretaking, these dynamics become amplified, often resulting in compulsive caretaking to the point of exhaustion. I have also encountered the opposite dynamic in which the failing health of partners who previously functioned as caretakers in their relationships forced the other partner to function autonomously for the first time, ironically providing an exciting sense of liberation.

As people age, they also become increasingly concerned about their own health and mortality, which may generate reflections on whether theirs was a life well-lived. Some seniors have deep regrets about relationships with their children, feeling remorse about having devoted excessive effort to their careers at the expense of meaningful family relationships. I have also known seniors whose relationships with their adult children have become permanently ruptured. These seniors experience a profound sense of loss, as well as despair, about their abject failure as parents. Even in the best of relationships, parents of adult children may experience what seems like unrequited love. Many seniors are prepared to drop everything when opportunities arise for spending time with their families. Their adult children, occupied with their own careers, children, and friends, perceive the situation rather differently. These seniors sometimes feel as if they are last in line for their adult children's time or energy. My friends who do not have daughters have confided that they feel especially vulnerable because it is often the women (daughters-in-law) who tend to control the family timetable. The parents of sons frequently feel they get the short end of the stick with their daughters-in-law, either choosing to live nearby or prioritizing their own parents in terms of family time.

Of course, the concerns clients bring to therapy may reach across various stages of Erikson's model and might not conform exactly to the timeline discussed above. However, Erik Erikson's eight stages of psychosocial development may serve as a useful framework in understanding common life struggles.

Conclusion

In this collection of essays, I hope to have put forth a useful compilation of common human struggles such that you, the reader, may begin to recognize how these issues might appear in your own life. The practice of clinical psychology is often one of pattern recognition, and this book is meant to help you identify solvable problems in your own life. It is my goal that by presenting examples from my clinical practice and from my own life, this book may provide invaluable insight into your own dynamics and relationships.

Acknowledgments

There are several people who deserve special recognition. Most importantly, I would like to mention the extraordinary role played by my husband Harry Greenspan, who was with me in every way throughout the writing of this collection of essays. This manuscript would not have been possible without him. A big debt of gratitude is owed to my dear friend of 50 years, Sandra Trehub, for her careful reading of multiple drafts, her perceptive editorial comments, as well as her unwavering enthusiasm for and faith in the value of its publication. She is a reader/editor extraordinaire. I would like to thank my amazing granddaughter, Jillian Troth, whose help was invaluable in competently editing, putting the finishing touches on the manuscript, and navigating its publication for her technologically challenged grandmother. I am also indebted to Rebecca Gradinger for her helpful suggestions regarding earlier drafts of the essays and her imbuing this project with significance.

I am deeply grateful to my many clients who shared their stories with me and who helped me understand the complexities of human nature. Likewise, I would like to acknowledge my colleagues, students and supervisees whose thought-provoking questions and stimulating discussions inspired many of these essays.

I am also fortunate to have been graced with the support and understanding of my children Johanna, Jeremy, and Michael, and my stepchildren Jonathan and Steven, as well as their spouses Sean, Joanne, Mascha, and Orly. They deserve much of the credit for the happy life I lead. My eleven grandchildren have nourished my spirit in more ways than I can express. I hope these pages can offer them some wisdom as they negotiate their own relationships. Finally, I want to express my appreciation for my late parents, Alice and David Zweig who encouraged me to always be the best version of myself.

References

1. Shea, V. (2013). Refrigerator Mother. In F. R. Volkmar (Ed.), *Encyclopedia of Autism Spectrum Disorders* (pp. 2532–2533). Springer. https://doi.org/10.1007/978-1-4419-1698-3_939
2. Levy, M. S. (2000). A Conceptualization of the Repetition Compulsion. *Psychiatry, 63*(1), 45–53. https://doi.org/10.1080/00332747.2000.11024893
3. Freud, S. (n.d.). Beyond the Pleasure Principle (C. J. M. Hubback, Trans.). *The International Psycho-Analytical Library, 4,* 55.
4. Miller, N. E. (1948). Theory and experiment relating psychoanalytic displacement to stimulus-response generalization. *The Journal of Abnormal and Social Psychology, 43*(2), 155–178. https://doi.org/10.1037/h0056728
5. Wachtel, P. L. (2014). An integrative relational point of view. *Psychotherapy, 51*(3), 342–349. https://doi.org/10.1037/a0037219
6. Lemche, E. (2020). Research evidence from

studies on filial imprinting, attachment, and early life stress: A new route for scientific integration. *Acta Ethologica, 23*(3), 127–133. https://doi.org/10.1007/s10211-020-00346-7

7. Gallagher, J. E. (1978). Sexual imprinting: Variables influencing the development of mate preference in Coturnix coturnix japonica. *Behavioral Biology, 24*(4), 481–491. https://doi.org/10.1016/S0091-6773(78)90843-X

8. Gallagher, J. E. (1977). Sexual imprinting: A sensitive period in Japanese quail (Coturnix coturnix japonica). *Journal of Comparative and Physiological Psychology, 91*(1), 72–78. https://doi.org/10.1037/h0077298

9. Aesop. (n.d.). *The Fox & the Grapes*. Library of Congress Aesop Fables. Retrieved June 28, 2021, from http://read.gov/aesop/005.html

10. Klein, M. (1957). Envy and Gratitude. In R. Money-Kyrle, B. Joseph, E. O'Shaughnessy, & H. Segal (Eds.), *Envy and Gratitude and Other Works 1946-1963* (Vol. 3, pp. 176–235). The Free Press. https://www.sas.upenn.edu/~cavitch/pdf-library/Klein_Envy_and_Gratitude.pdf

11. Elworthy, F. T. (1895). *The evil eye. An account of this ancient and wide spread superstition* (7th ed.). J. Murray. http://archive.org/details/evileyeaccountof00elwo

12. McEwan, I. (2002). *Atonement*. Vintage Canada.

13. Doka, K. J. (1989). Disenfranchised grief. In *Disenfranchised grief: Recognizing hidden sorrow* (pp. 3–11). Lexington Books/D. C. Heath and Com.

14. Freud, S. (1923). *The Ego and the Id.*

https://docs.google.com/viewerng/viewer?
url=https://www.sigmundfreud.net/the-ego-
and-the-id.pdf

15. Lifton, R. J. (1980). The concept of the
survivor. In J. E. Dimsdale (Ed.), *Survivors,
Victims, and Perpetrators: Essays on the Nazi Holocaust*
(pp. 113–126). Hemisphere.

16. Chapman, G. (2015). *The 5 Love Languages.*
Northfield Publishing.

17. ten Boom, C. (1982). *Clippings from My Notebook.*
Thomas Nelson Inc.

18. Freud, S. (1916). Some Character-Types Met
with in Psycho-Analytic Work. *The Standard
Edition of the Complete Works of Sigmund Freud, 14,*
309–333.

19. Walls, J. (2006). *The Glass Castle.* Scribner Book
Company.

20. Vance, J. D. (2016). *Hillbilly Elegy.* Harper.

21. Westover, T. (2018). *Educated.* Random House.

22. Berglas, S., & Jones, E. E. (1978). Drug choice
as a self-handicapping strategy in response to
noncontingent success. *Journal of Personality and
Social Psychology, 36*(4), 405–417.
https://doi.org/10.1037/0022-3514.36.4.405

23. Kohut, H., & Wolf, E. S. (1978). The Disorders
of the Self and their Treatment: An Outline.
The International Journal of Psycho-Analysis, 59,
413–425.

24. Ogden, T. H. (1979). On Projective
Identification. *The International Journal of Psycho-
Analysis, 60,* 357–373.

25. Fromm, E. (1964). *The Heart of Man: Its Genius
for Good and Evil.* Harper & Row.

26. Kernberg, O. F. (1984). *Severe Personality Disorders: Psychotherapeutic Strategies*. Yale University Press.

27. Kernberg, O. F. (1975). *Borderline conditions and pathological narcissism*. Jason Aronson.

28. Gottman, J. M., Coan, J., Carrere, S., & Swanson, C. (1998). Predicting Marital Happiness and Stability from Newlywed Interactions. *Journal of Marriage and the Family, 60*, 5–22.

29. Frost, R. (1874-1963). *Revelation*. Retrieved July 4, 2021, from https://poets.org/poem/revelation

30. q0j0p. (2010, April 10). *Urban Dictionary: Shit Sandwich*. Urban Dictionary. https://www.urbandictionary.com/define.php?term=Shit%20Sandwich

31. Erikson, E. H. (1994). *Identity and the Life Cycle*. W. W. Norton & Company.

32. Erikson, E. H. (1994). *Insight and Responsibility*. W. W. Norton & Company.

33. Erikson, E. H. (1998). *The Life Cycle Completed*. W. W. Norton & Company.

34. Bowlby, J. (1977). The Making and Breaking of Affectional Bonds. *British Journal Of Psychiatry, 130*, 201–210.

35. Malan, D. (1995). *Individual Psychotherapy and the Science of Psychodynamics* (2nd ed.). Butterworth-Heinemann.